LOVE IS A PLACE

Joan Margarit was born in 1938 in Sanaüja, La Segarra region, in Catalonia. He is an architect, and from 1968 until his retirement was also Professor of Structural Calculations at Barcelona's Technical School of Architecture, working for part of that time on Gaudi's Sagrada Familia cathedral. He first published poetry in Spanish, but after four books decided to write in Catalan. From 1980 he began to establish his reputation as a major Catalan poet. As well as publishing many collections in Catalan, he has published Spanish versions of all his work, and over the past 15 years has gained recognition as a leading poet in Spanish. In 2008 he received the Premio Nacional de Poesía del Estado Español, Spain's highest literary award, for his collection *Casa de Misericòrdia*, as well as the Premi Nacional de Literatura de la Generalitat de Catalunya. In 2013 he was awarded Mexico's Premio de Poetas del Mundo Latino Víctor Sandoval for all his poetry.

Tugs in the Fog: Selected Poems (Bloodaxe Books, 2006), translated by Anna Crowe, the first English translation of his Catalan poetry, was a Poetry Book Society Recommended Translation. *Strangely Happy*, a selection of later poems from *Casa de Misericòrdia* (2007) and *Misteriosament feliç* (2008), also translated by Anna Crowe, was published by Bloodaxe in 2011. A third translation by Anna Crowe of his most recent poetry, *Love Is a Place* (Bloodaxe Books, 2016), includes all the poems from three Catalan collections: *No era lluny ni difícil* (It Wasn't Far Away or Difficult, 2010), *Es perd el senyal* (The Signal Is Fading, 2012) and *Estimar és un lloc* (From Where to Begin to Love Again, 2014).

JOAN MARGARIT

Love Is a Place

TRANSLATED BY
ANNA CROWE

BLOODAXE BOOKS

ISBN: 978 1 78037 328 7

First published 2016 by
Bloodaxe Books Ltd,
Eastburn,
South Park,
Hexham,
Northumberland NE46 1BS.

www.bloodaxebooks.com
For further information about Bloodaxe titles
please visit our website or write to
the above address for a catalogue.

Supported using public funding by
ARTS COUNCIL
ENGLAND

Cover design: Neil Astley & Pamela Robertson-Pearce.

Printed in Great Britain by Bell & Bain Limited, Glasgow, Scotland, on
acid-free paper sourced from mills with FSC chain of custody certification.

ACKNOWLEDGEMENTS

Love Is a Place is a translation by Anna Crowe of Joan Margarit's three most recent Catalan collections: *No era lluny ni difícil* (It Wasn't Far Away or Difficult, 2010), *Es perd el senyal* (The Signal Is Fading, 2012) and *Estimar és un lloc* (From Where to Begin to Love Again, 2014), all published by Edicions Proa S.A., Barcelona. The translation of this work was supported by a grant from the Institut Ramon Llull.

 **institut ramon llull**
Catalan Language and Culture

CONTENTS

Second book:

THE SIGNAL IS FADING (2012)

Third book:
FROM WHERE TO BEGIN TO LOVE AGAIN (2014)

FOREWORD

I love these poems for many reasons. When I first read Joan Margarit, I heard a powerfully distinctive voice, a spirit of great freedom and energy, humaneness, mischief, and depth.

In these naked, subtle, clear poems, surprise and wisdom are often right next to each other. There is often a doubleness going on in a poem – lots of pairs of ions, the magnetic positives and negatives which hold matter together. This gives his poems a sense of naturally occurring disorder and order, and a welcome absence of wilful craft. There is an exhilarating sense of the spontaneous, the organic – of happenstance and chance. And at the end of a good number of his poems I have the desire to scream – as at a theorem proved, or a victory.

Joan Margarit's work is fierce, and it is partisan – it is on the side of fresh perception. He's a fierce protector of his precise truth, like the bees – like a big bee – with honey. His abstractions and his daily objects are given to the reader with equal, deft, homemade tenderness and brio.

Often, at the beginning, a Joan Margarit poem will locate us. 'It was a top-floor flat.' Many poems start up quietly, from within an ordinary situation. And then, suddenly, we're in deep, off-beat thought and feeling. And a Joan Margarit poem often has a turn at the end, as well as a reversal – sometimes a double reversal. Reading him, we are in the world of history, wit, imagination, dream, and memory. At the same time, it is the plain real intransigent world.

What is so unusual in Margarit's work? I think it is the juxtaposition of the everyday syntax with his intimacy and wisdom – the combination of clarity and accurate subtlety which honours the basic mysteriousness (unknowability) of life.

I love Margarit's frankness – sexuality a part of life like food, sleep, death, health, illness – and his unflinchingness. He's stoical – and singing. And defenceless – but for basic human integrity and dignity.

Joan Margarit has what I've heard some great quarterbacks have – equal ability to turn in any direction at any moment. I think samurai have that. I think in U.S. football it's called 'broken field'. There is a lot of change of direction within these poems – and many moments of Satori! The experience of reading him feels the way consciousness itself feels.

Each of Margarit's poems is its own being, like a living creature with its own body-shape and voice, its own breath and heartbeat. His poems live and breathe in their natural habitat. They are elegant and shapely. And sometimes they seem almost overheard, as if they are singing in the voice the mind uses when talking with itself or with its close close other. It is common enough speech, and it is brilliant, too, sensually beautiful (but not too beautiful) and with a genuine, just-conceived feeling. Those of you who know Joan Margarit's work, welcome to its most recent incarnation! Those who are coming to it for the first time – it's good to have your company. Here is our brother, his genius quietly electric on the page.

SHARON OLDS

It Wasn't Far Away or Difficult

(2010)

It wasn't far away or difficult

The time has come
when life that is lost no longer hurts,
when lust is a useless light
and envy forgotten. It is a time
of wise and necessary losses,
it is not a time for arriving, but for going away.
It is now that love
finally coincides with intelligence.
It wasn't far away or difficult.
It is a time that leaves me only the horizon
with which to measure solitude.
The time of protective sadness.

Strolling

He enjoys strolling about the streets by himself,
hands behind his back, in no hurry,
among the early morning people and cars.
A serious child,
he has been obedient all his life.
Now he steps out from behind
the one who for years disguised him as a man.
There are a few things that have not changed,
brief, gentle things, like the absences
which the first lamps illumine at dusk.
He remembers when they explained to the child
who has now returned that the dead were in heaven.
That heaven which is sometimes so blue,
and so cold the further it is from earth,
so black when the stars up there come on.
The child returns and takes him by the hand.
Both of them move away
until they are a dot in the sky. Birds of passage.

Love will have the final word

It was a top-floor flat.
At night, standing in front of the window,
gazing down at the city, he was thinking:
If from behind she should see me
I might inspire her with confidence
in the helmsman at the ship's prow.
But it was nothing more than a city at night.
Their long life together. And now he felt
that it had all been something he had made up,
an order previous to something
that had never come to pass.
It might have been about some old misunderstanding.
A house that had burned down in which each
lights his own lamp.
He went on undressing: it was all written
in that old man's body in the mirror.
There was nothing else. Love would have
from now on the final word.
And, silently, he began to weep.

Classicism

When I did my military service I was declared
a first-class shot. I took aim
thinking that I was on the edge of an abyss,
with my back turned, and my heels over the void.
As I fired, I closed my eyes,
gazing at a place deep inside me.
Life erased that story
until one night forty years later,
in the twilight of the room
in which our daughter lay dying.
With what rage did I close my eyes
in that despairing coitus.
That's why now I live in a place
where only money counts,
just enough to buy a solitude
that resembles love. And which perhaps is love.

Dry-stone walls

The path, open and flat as it goes through the wood,
when it comes out under the open sky turns hostile,
invaded by shrubs and brambles,
and starts to go downhill until, at the very bottom,
it ends in a ploughed field, really well-ploughed
and without a single weed. A path
still bordered and protected by
a dry-stone wall with its freestone blocks,
enormous some of them, well-positioned,
without mortar, bare-boned, each in its place.

Only one who feels a defencelessness
so deep that it reaches into the here and now
could raise up with his hands a wall
that retains such strength.
Someone who, walking towards nothingness,
was building a wall to protect a path
leading to a final, and maybe magnificent order.

Penultimate poem to my mother

With the war over, we would play in the street,
and on hearing a plane you would come out to find us
until the sound was lost beyond the clouds.
These are the ruins of that safe place
that once was there for childhood.
One morning, I got up
very early, and you were in the dark,
sitting at the kitchen table
just like a gull in the cleft
of a rock during a storm.

All I see is the tiny light of a house
that is no longer there,
but it makes me feel less wretched.
Until the danger is lost on the horizon.

Shutting up the beach apartment

It's all clean and tidy now.
The wardrobes closed, the windows too.
We haven't forgotten anything on top of the furniture.
The bedroom with the bed made,
the bedside table with the picture
of the girl with her eyes lit
by a smile.
By herself all winter and listening to the sea.

Poetry, a ballad

I have built the structures of buildings.
Structures of iron
which ice makes dangerous.
Life has gone on lingering under the chill
of winters on building sites,
and I have gone on growing old seeing the sun
rise with hammer blows behind the girders.
Now I see it come up behind another structure
that rises svelte and naked, as though it were a woman
I have always loved. When I touch it,
it is icy, and burns me while I continue
with what never stops: building.

The darker part of the path

I went down to the garden very early
and, like lance-points, the stars were marking
the distant and exact siege of forgetting.
When I went out into the chill beneath the trees,
a fox saw me, and stopped
on the shadowy lawn.
The two of us stood motionless
for a few moments, staring at each other
and then, without haste, it went off
towards the darker part of the path.
I saw in its eyes the mystery in my own
and I think that at another time as well,
crossing a lawn one night,
I entered another garden where I surprised
with my glance another pair of eyes.
Something is being sought after. For all I know,
nothing but dignity.
That of life while it goes off gradually
towards the darker part of the path.

Raquel

They taught you to do everything really properly.
Playing obediently, you became used
to the safe places which one day would fail you.
Order is as dangerous as disorder,
they are the locked rooms of childhood
and at the same time the draughts, the slamming doors
in a house where nobody now lives.
With a shy smile you come from a long way off,
from your peaceful black and white world
with a mother and a coal-burning stove
and a gallery with thin window glass
through which the heat of one weather escaped
towards the cold blue sky of an island courtyard.
You started to become used
to not trusting yourself. To not knowing
you had done something wrong so that you could come back
with swear words you didn't utter
and scornful gestures that weren't you.
Loving is something you did well,
but as for life, how much death it brought
to your hard eyes which have now gone back
to expressing the shy tenderness
of that well-behaved girl in black and white
who learned to do everything properly and well,
so that she could save our love all these years later.

I'll wait for you here

When he wakes, before he gets out of bed
he winds his wristwatch –
the old model that they took to the moon,
in nineteen sixty-nine.
He has felt how the arthritis in his hands
has recorded a harder time.
The unforeseen erection has brought him
the humiliating image of the key:
the young men pushed it, thick and heavy,
into a pocket when they went dancing. The girl,
when she felt it, slid to the other side,
where another key was waiting for her
eager to open the most difficult lock.
That's how it was, back then.
The time of his youth.
He doesn't smile when he thinks of it. He knows
the pain hands inflict, winding time's clock.
The force of silence doesn't change,
nor do the world's laws. He also knows that now
no woman would want to dance with him.
And he resigns himself to it. But he doesn't smile.

Tunnel

The wood and the blue sky surround it.
Light sinks in rock
as though down the barrel of a gun.
Surrounded by the warm, damp darkness –
an enormous, sheltering cellar – I remember
the carriage lit up inside the tunnel.
From my childhood there still echoes
the iron tenderness of those trains
as harsh and hard as knowledge.
This knowledge that now allows me
to look ahead without regret
to the mouth of bright light approaching me.

The explanation

In the early morning, at the time when the streets
are full of children going to school,
you can feel how the air has another dignity.

There are some who go to small schools with a garden
and teachers who never raise their voice to them.
Children with difficult movements,
as though remembering somebody lost in the air.
Their parents, often, weep when they are alone.

You need so much time to understand. That is because
there are never two chances.
But these children will never know that,
I tell myself, thinking of that smile
and aware, with anguish, of how it is fading.
A few memories are all that now remain
to explain to myself
that love is where I have left my life.

The origins of tragedy

God, who is the most brutal of all myths,
would not save me even from myself,
because he is a cul-de-sac:
in attributing feelings to him we lose
the mystery, his only strength.
I imagine him as a cemetery
for cars, God's. Remains, carcases,
a scattering of metaphysical bits and pieces.
Myths are this brightness
behind which we shut everything dark.
They come from some deep error of memory. Living,
from beginning to end, means searching for consolation.
Searching for it in the pain words have.
In the grey music of the rain.
In this military weariness of the wind.
In the sky with no oxygen from the past.
It wasn't far away or difficult. It was nothing more
than this epic poem with no epic.
Nietzsche was wrong:
the weaker the myths, the stronger we are.

Resources

The terrace of the bar when evening falls
faces a violet blue horizon
of gentle mountains. Beside me,
three men are shouting. Offensive, cocksure.
The arrogance of ignorance, at once
so harsh and natural, like death.
I gaze at the clean, indifferent silence
of the greens and carmines the horizon paints,
and I remember Vlaminck and Millet.
But the shouting voices rain blows on me,
they are a hard and sad hammer within.
And then melancholy comes to my rescue.
A melancholy that impels me
towards an intimate, far-off place.
I have done this since I was very young. I am there,
contemplating the horizon with those I have loved
but whom I have now lost. With them alone.

Young ones in the night

It isn't history I feel nostalgic for.
It's geography.
For how it was that night in the seaside town
we saw from a bar in Vallvidrera.
There is a time for grief: it is the same
as for joy.
A time like a torrent
that gives way to the time for sadness.
There is no precipice, no sigh
I might not have been able to foresee.

It isn't history I feel nostalgic for.
It's geography.
For how it was that night on a coast
with no houses for as far as we could see.
The strength of the waves could be felt.
The smell of the sea was the smell of the night,
and in the stars we saw a refuge.
We didn't realise we were contemplating
the black rump of time's horse.
It isn't history I feel nostalgic for.
It's geography.

Vallvidrera: a hill behind the city from which you can gaze down on Barcelona
and the sea.

Deer

While the blue sky is reflected in the gorge,
on one of the banks I make ready for the leap,
which may be the last, from one rock to another.
It all depends on the air and the thrust.
The young deer is frightened of death
because it has not realised how little
anyone's life weighs.

Buoys

From the beach, I am standing, watching you
while you swim far out towards the buoys.
You have made a pact with the serene to-ing and fro-ing
that rocks them and carries you,
in your watertight dark goggles,
towards the paths of the sea
that you lost in childhood.
Swimming you penetrate the depths of a myth
that shuts me out until sex
may become just like dead seaweed.
And then I will be the last buoy
towards which you will one day swim.

Coming out of a cinema

Remembering old cinemas is never sad,
because they were an illusion
that will never become a lie.
The film's feeble web of light
has lingered for a few instants in my eyes.
The women of air and shadow have gone,
but they leave me some of their smiles
so that I don't have to go back alone
to this place of everything that has never existed.

Old man on the beach

Ferocious summer floods the whole space.
With my gaze sliding over breasts and belly,
towards the pubis of this young woman,
a brutal longing is dazzling me.
And suddenly, blinded by the brightness,
I feel as though I had stopped on the threshhold
of a house in darkness.
Trying to make my eyes
adjust to this new gloom.

Metaphysical tale

There was once a lonely man
who loved a woman who is not.
It was night in the quiet city:
walking along the streets while he looked
at the lit windows, the black sky,
he asked the woman who is not:
what do you feed on?
And she told him: on lost pain.
Now he is a man who is not.
Wrapped in the coldness of his love,
he looks at loneliness, which has become
the only real thing, and of a great tenderness.

A place

It wasn't far away. Nor was it difficult.
What is far away and difficult is the coast
I leave behind and which I will never see again.
An innocent disaster keeps silent
in this myth of a useless past.
Which is brutally useless.
So much so, it is as though it were false. Brutally false.

The place that now surrounds me is far out at sea.
It is a sad place, but truly so.
There comes a light wind forcing a passage
from yesterday bringing me that utterly beautiful
Weep, oh weep, which, like the sea, resonates
in the 'Song of Return'. We are lost.

'Song of Return': Well-known poem by the great Catalan poet, Joan Maragall
(1860-1911), about the return of a warship with defeated troops, in the Spanish-
United States war of 1898.

Last poem to my mother

Your job was not in the light,
but further back, in the half light.
Tired of being a mother. Desiring
an oblivion that you had already arranged.
I take the last steps through this
desolate encampment of my poems.
Where did the love come from that taught
me an honest way of making verses?

Lyric at 70

Let no one search in this lyric
for the big bonfires of the solstices.
It is philosophers who kindle them,
and religions, but they provide no warmth
for the cold there is in metaphysics,
which is the same as in superstition.

If in this cold you have to burn your life,
go back to the hard soil.
Put up with the one you have been
and do not go meekly into winter.
The woman you quarrel with
lies, just as you do, about the past.
Sad in her wind, she loves you while cursing you.
Yet do not go meekly into winter.

Suffering

Evening grows darker inside the hospital.
All around, broad and empty streets,
the lit windows of the suburbs.
In the Accident & Emergencies corridor I saw
our helplessness in your eyes.

We didn't emerge from there till the early hours.
It was all over. You smile. Tired,
we drive home among the lorries on the motorway.
What a hard happiness it is, that of the traffic lights.

Now my eyes are free in the night,
but so much pain comes that they are already wary.
They are wary, as well, even while they protect.
There is too much death in these eyes.

The sun on a portrait

I am looking at a photograph
on which a ray of sun is glancing.
So much talking and so much arguing
while our love was slipping away from us.
No logic can cross the abyss
there is between saying I love you and not saying it.
I smile in front of the photograph.
We love for a long time.
How reluctant it is to leave portraits, the sun.

The heaviest hour

In the window there is the morning star
shining steadily in the black sky.
The bar below has not yet opened,
and all that can be heard are the mild waves
and the sad, timid song of the first bird.

I have gone on being solitary like all those
who have never loved their mistakes.
As a young man, the biggest one I made
was not imagining to myself that soon
would come unknown cruelties.
And it's this they speak of, the slow waves.
A train can be heard passing above the roof tops,
over the iron bridge that crosses the village.
A cry of despairing love.
A sad tenderness that's departing.

Architect in Las Palmas

Your face still smiles at me, youthful
from every street.
I had never been back since I was a boy.
I saw – burnished by the air of the Atlantic –
the bell tower transparent with happiness
and the huge arch, in its calm, of the market.
A new clemency appears
in these buildings if I imagine
when they were simply ideas inside you.
I understand the enthusiasm of those days,
the generosity of an old profession.
Your more tranquil period begins here,
for nowhere did you attain dignity
as you did on this island. Here
where inside me, at last, you may rest.

Couple

Nobody comes along it any more, the path
we see from the house. Grass grows over it:
now there are only nervous blackbirds
pecking at quiet absence.
It's a path of no return. The house
endures slowly and, very often,
muffled in mist.
Here inside, memory turns welcoming.
Welcoming and sad, for nothing
protects as sadness can.

Love now means gazing out of the windows,
for the past is a holiday
for us alone.

The Holocaust Museum, Jerusalem

I went inside into the darkness of the great vault
where all the tiny lights of dead children
were trembling as in a night sky.
A voice was reciting, never ceasing,
the list of their names, a prayer
so sad no God has ever heard its like.
I thought of Joana. Dead children
are always inside that same darkness
where memories are lights and the lights are tears.
I am too old not to weep for them all.
I have constructed buildings like cattle trucks
with skeletons of iron. Huge trucks
that will one day come back and drag people
off to an end they already picture.
Because everyone has seen the truth,
merely a gleam on a puddle of dirty water.
The hall of the dead children is inside me.
I am too old not to weep for them all.

Reading

It has made me enter into other lives.
For days I've been reading, but today
I raise my eyes. I scarcely know a thing
about the person who wrote this book.
I am ashamed to know of them only
their lucidity. Survival
is nothing more than this kind
of conversation in silence and outside time.
This is terrifying
and goes on in the mind's abyss,
that cold blue sky where love is
the only shape posterity takes.

Street at night in Santa Coloma

Beneath the pavement there must still exist
that track with its verges of brambles
covered in dust and laden with blackberries.
They were the fields of a suburb where we lived
side by side, after the war, the poorest
among both losers and those who had won.

The rusty glow of some evenings
dies away while I gaze
at the lights of the shops reflected in the asphalt
that erased that track forever.

It has the hardness of the unknown:
solid and filthy, one of time's pavements
trampled by so many unremembering feet.
Dusty shoes wear it away,
compacting and steamrollering oblivion
until my childhood lies buried.
It is the same madness
of warming oneself in the fire without flames
that I can kindle on any old street.

Evening

When the waters of time have settled,
because your stone is already at the bottom,
we still go on
gazing at the corner of the small living-room
where, eight years today, you are no longer.
I see how, made of nothing
but time, you come back in the evening air.
But, in truth, where are you now?
And you, with a smile, point
at your mother who, closing her book,
rises and smiles at me also and turns on the light.

A History

A hundred years of war, my grandmother repeated:
she was a child living in a village where every night
she heard people fighting in the streets.
And she would tell me, as though it were a story,
about the day the soldiers dragged
her mother away to be shot at dawn
against the cemetery wall.
When I listened to her, I too was a child,
and my father, a soldier in a detention centre.

From those days no threat now reaches me.
They are a long way off, those dead,
tired of playing the part of the dead.
We have chosen to be a nation without heroes.
Justly, this is our strength today.
We have to erase all those myths that are hidden
beneath the imperturbable gaze
of the birds of prey still keeping watch.
All my life I have had to look at them,
made of stone or bronze on those huge scutcheons
presiding over the façades of the State.
The body facing the front,
the head in stern profile.
Their wings, a cloak over their shoulder.
A malevolent eye, the cruel beak about
to tear out entrails. Dominating
and never sleeping. What air do you breathe,
you colossal birds with talons,
to decide what you call unity of fate?
I rather think you have become old, as I have.

That your gaze now is neither harsh, nor fierce. Nor predatory.
But that farmyard smell
still lingers. The smell of chicken shit.
That hymn. The History of Spain.

May '68

In the rainy Paris to which I return
I find nothing now but dead leaves.
They trail along on the asphalt
with which public order has covered
the boulevards of pink paving-stones.
Here the corpse of the French chanson burns.
The city I loved I have lost:
It remains only in the river, in the glitter
of a wake that a barge leaves.
Paris cannot be anywhere but in my eyes.
I do not have to write it any more poems.

Mothers calling

The city used to end here. I lived
in this building, at that time among building sites
and roads without houses. When evening
deepens its indifferent blues,
the past can be heard like a sax
playing, listlessly, to oblivion.

In the dusk, hearing that voice
that called to me from a long way off,
I was no longer afraid to go home alone
through empty lots that still I'm crossing,
repressing as then the old impulse,
now that it's dark, to carry on playing.

Anniversary with statue

Memories get mixed up with the rain
and slide down the face
made of marble half-hidden amongst the ivy.
I think that today the pity is greater
through the green ambush of the rain
that this morning brings you close into the courtyard.
I look at the marble face. It is telling me
that the promised land was death.

Breast cancer

She has looked at herself in the mirror
with the future in her face and with fury
pouring from her hard eyes.
The wig is there, nicely-combed
and sitting on top of a model head.
She remembers that doll with red hair
that she buried in the garden.
She seizes the wig and beats it angrily.
Hair is working its way through on her head
like hoar frost in winter.
That unkind child is the one who has saved her.

Fragments

From what dark place inside me
do two magpies silently fly away?
We were young, travelling by car
and, as we came round a bend
we saw them there on the tarmac,
pecking furiously at a dead dog.
Just at the last moment and without haste
they flew up unfolding the elegant
black and white of their plumage.
We said nothing – you were driving
and made a gesture of disgust.

I have never forgotten it. If I look at you,
still in the depths of your eyes, slowly,
two magpies silently fly away.
I love what is left to us:
this nuptial flight and the carrion.

They will want you to die

You hear this calm evening sea,
half organ, half cello.
It grows dark. Like all the old, you keep watch
over your approaching end, while all along the beach
the sea is a piece of silk unfolding.
You listen to what the breaking waves tell you:
that those who will love you, will want you to die.
Because you will love them, you will want to die.
The implacable logic of love.
The implacable logic of death.
The relief that comes from knowing they are so close together.

What sustains me

I have gone on building
the common sense of my refuge.
I live there with sadness
and happiness,
implacable neighbours.
It has been a good refuge,
and you somewhere,
so close and so far away.
Now that I am old, love
still takes me by surprise:
like going into a dark,
empty casino where, suddenly,
all the lights have come on.

What kind of lives

It's a large cup, of English china
with a rustic decoration.
It sits on a shelf in the kitchen.
Every day my father breakfasted from it:
an object about which all I know
is that it came from the last days of the war,
in the middle of the retreat towards France,
perhaps from a ransacked house, who knows.
He never said anything more about it. Something
bound him forever to this cup:
gratitude or fear, guilt perhaps.
There is nobody left, now, whom I can ask.

There are, on the china, some words
I cannot translate, in antiquated English.
And, for so many mornings, my father's lips
drinking milk with cocoa, those leftover
pieces of bread, the brown crumbs
that remained in the bottom. Like him now.
What kind of lives are these lives of ours
that the wind carries off like poison gas?
Like the body's ashes, all the past
blown into a bowl that no longer has any use.

Sailing alone

A moonless night for the man
who has come to search for peace from the sea.
There's a light in the cabin, no one on deck.
Moored on its starboard side to the pontoon,
the yacht moves gently to and fro
on the black velvet water
like a horse shut in a stable.
The man cannot sleep. He listens to the stays
and shrouds, how they moan when the mast
leans with a sinister lapping.
Life is like the sea, that pens him
in ports that are ever more far away.
More meaningless.
And often there is no other light
that that of his sailing boat. That's home.

Twilight

Life's cellar in your eyes has gazed
each summer at the vines with their purple grapes,
smooth as the skin of twilight.
Those were days whose sky was fragile
with bird cries
and children's voices.
Each of us was changing
as must does, silently, slowly,
towards knowledge.
Wine is time, it has the rough taste of time.
A bottle of wine can be home.
Hatred as much as love are both inside it.
Once it is emptied, the lees of forgetting.

Halley's Comet at Forès

Leaving the car with the headlights turned off,
we walked forward a few paces into a field.
The night was a coal about to catch light,
and Joana was holding on to us tightly.
The comet high above,
a stranger crossing the night sky.
What damned wish could we ask for,
when the most innocent of the three
is now further away from us than Halley's Comet?
That will come back again and again,
weaving this web, sometimes of love,
around what were once our lives.

Like the seagulls

Crossing storms,
you learn to plane
flying over life.
To move forward using
the wind's violence.
Like the seagulls.

Those times

I was born – forgive me – , in the age
of the pergola and of tennis.

JAIME GIL DE BIEDMA

Like every other day, when it's still dark,
I take the car to go and swim.
It's cold and raining. I drive along
surrounded by the dance of other headlights
behind the veil of rain of the streets.

The car park is between the swimming pool
and the tennis courts. It's beginning to be day.
I get out of the car, and on the ground I see
the tennis ball, covered
in soft wool and soaking wet.
It is a huge yellow pearl
on top of the paving stones that now glisten,
hard and varnished by the rain.

Taking me by surprise, a memory
comes back from the blue skies
of a grey and affectionate poverty graced by
neither pergolas nor tennis. The ball,
what joy if I had found it,
so sumptuous as it seemed to me,
as much as, now, the rain humiliates it.

My loneliness, like the ball's,
has long ago lost its prestige.
On the ground of the car park
I see all that I've loved and won't be able
to save any longer from the cold or the rain.

SECOND BOOK

The Signal Is Fading

(2012)

The signal is fading

Don't pity the man you have been,
because pity is too brief:
It doesn't give you time to build anything there.
At night, in a small airport,
you watch a plane taking off.
The signal is gradually fading.
You feel the conviction that you are living
through years with no hope that are already
the happiest of your life.
There is another poetry, there always will be,
just as there is another music.
That of the deaf Beethoven. When the signal is fading.

Poetry

Just as it was for Sisyphus,
life for me is this rock.
I take it up and carry it to the very top.
When it falls I go back to searching for it
and, grasping it in my arms,
I heft it once again.
It is a form of hope.
I think I would have been a sadder man
if I'd never been able to heft a rock
with no more motive than for love.
Carrying it for love's sake to the very top.

An old woman

She has read every novel
that speaks about couples or about mothers and daughters.
Love stories, therefore.
She hasn't a whisker of belief in any god,
she doesn't believe in anything but people.
When I come along with my cynical views,
she listens to me and grows sad. I have realised
how much I still desire her, but she
regards my love as being far from passion,
perhaps through so much death, through having had
a full but difficult life: tremendously full
at times. I haven't understood her well enough
and don't know enough of what she has understood about me.
But there is a refuge for both of us.
And I enjoy a privilege: I carry
her poem written in my glance.
I wouldn't know how to write a poem at all like her.

Having had supper

I hear a ring at the door and go to open it,
but there's nobody.
I think of those whom I love and who won't return.
I don't close the door but maintain my welcome.
With my hand on the door frame, I wait.
Life goes on settling itself in pain
as houses do on their foundations.
And I know for whom I linger leaving a sheaf
of hospitable light in the empty street.

Withdrawal

It was unknown to me, this pleasure
in obedience to a law.
Here I stay, where life has carried me.
I walk about the city and feel myself a foreigner there.
I don't understand the friends who've grown old with me
and no longer know what to talk about with them.
Each new couple my children compose seems even stranger.
I don't remember ever having longed
so urgently for solitude.
These are signals. An animal knows them and pays heed.
You have to really search to find a dead fox,
a dead wild boar. First, they hide.

Singing of that damned anger (1938)

The thing that frightened me most,
I don't know if it was the war or giving birth.
She described it to me so many times
it's almost as though I remembered it myself.
She must have wanted something from me.
Maybe that I should love her after she was dead.

Drought accords well with growing old

It accords with what you have sown not sprouting.
The discipline of a futile task
and the hope of hearing how rain
falls into into the word *dark*.
Suddenly I see my own death
that is here in the room with me:
It has stopped to look a photograph.
It does not speak to me. If you don't miss the past,
death has nothing to speak about.

A structure

When I was a young man
I built a dome made of iron.
A few months ago they demolished it.
Looked at from the place where it's ending,
life appears absurd.
But its meaning comes from forgiveness.
Each time I think more and more
about forgiveness. Already I live in its shadow.
Forgiveness for a dome made of iron.
Forgiveness for those who pulled it down.

A village

My mother was a schoolteacher.
We lived on our own, the two of us.
We didn't even have a lavatory.
Above the house, the stars
playing in the eyes of a child
who sits on a urinal outside in the yard.

She was humiliated and frightened.
At midday she had to lock herself
inside the school to escape
the siege by that vile
falangist mayor of Rubí.
I was a winter bush in a corner
of my mother's big grey eyes.

Falangist: member of the Spanish Fascist Party, equivalent to the brown shirts
and black shirts of Hitler and Mussolini.

People at the beach

The woman parks the car in a street beside the sand.
She gets out and, slowly, takes out and unfolds
the wheelchair. Afterwards, she lifts the boy,
sits him down and puts his legs straight.
She pushes a few stray locks of hair from her face,
and, aware of her skirt billowing about,
starts pushing the chair towards the sea.
She reaches the beach along some wooden planks,
but the planks stop several yards from the sea.
Nearby, the lifeguard stares at the sea.
The woman lifts the boy out: she grasps him
under his arms and, her back to the water,
walks dragging him while his feet
leave two sad tracks in the sand.
She has brought him to where the waves reach,
she has left him on the sand and gone back
to fetch the sunshade and the wheelchair.

The last few yards. There are always
these cursed, terrible last few yards.
They are the ones that will break your heart.
There is no love in the sand. Nor in the sun.
Nor in the wooden planks, nor in the eyes
of the lifeguard, nor in the sea. Love
is these last few yards. Their loneliness.

Foreigner

While operating a searchlight
on a warship, Wittgenstein pondered
questions of symbolic logic.
Everything can be confused with truth
but the noise from the depths that history makes
warns me that I belong to my time,
and that it's only there that the key
to deciphering horror is to be found.
We have lost little but we have lost it all.
I still have a searchlight
so that I don't forget who I am or my time:
the romantic existentialism whence I come –
the *Iliad* in my veins, and the Bible,
brutal, dramatic, the worst of me.

Six years old

The candle, the sparks from the stove
and my sister in the cradle,
where she would die before dawn.
The winter night devours angels,
but that was home: my father and mother
came in with the cold clinging to their overcoats.
The doctor ordered her to be bathed in water with ice.

Once the tiny body had been shrouded,
they put me to bed.
While they were covering me up, I comforted them
saying: *You've still got me.*

Life and poetry

Maybe everything happens outside. Maybe the inside
is an angel-less engine-room,
Maybe love means washing the dishes
or else ironing a dirty shirt.
And the rest a few gusts
of bad temper that come like the wind.
Maybe inside there are only
a handful of red lights and the hum
of machinery. The poems.

Dignity

If despair has the force
of logical certainty,
and envy a timetable as secret
as an army train, we are lost.
Castilian stifles me and I do not hate it.
It is not to be blamed for its strength:
for my weakness, even less.
Yesterday it was a well-structured language
for thinking in, for making pacts, for dreaming,
and which nobody now speaks:
a subconscious of loss and greed
in which the finest songs ring out.
The present is the language of the streets,
abused and adulterated, clinging on
like ivy to the ruins of history.
It is the language in which I write.
It is also a well-structured language
for thinking in, for making pacts, for dreaming.
And the old songs will be saved.

5th of January '43

Well covered-up in bed,
I'm wrapped in the darkness and silence
in which the war has ended,
and I confuse them with the darkness and silence
that there is on the Night of the Three Kings.

What a clear darkness I remember.
Where life ends,
nights are sometimes still like that.

The flag

At night I am like a child's drawing,
beside the moon, on top of a building.
An echo of cannon and horses
comes from the history books,
empty places where I was a symbol
before I was nothing, colours on a cloth
abandoned to the sudden hatred of the wind.

I see you early in the morning,
when a window lights up in a courtyard.
Don't deceive yourselves: only thus are you
truth, defenceless, going into a lavatory.
I don't understand either what unites us or what you expect
from me or from the wind after so much time.

Learning in the street

Along the paving stones of dusk,
beneath the red and black cathedral,
beside the river's filthy waters, I learned
to be grateful. Provincial city:
how much delight I stole from you.
And though your name brings me
no echo of any love story, to you I owe
what I know of beauty.
The heaps of dry leaves welcomed
those that went on falling
ruddy and slow from the plane trees.
I walked, plunged up to my knees,
in the sea of leaves that was the Devesa,
cathedral of autumn for a boy
who went there to play during school hours
and learned that nothing was a game.

There is a silence that I can hear still.
I plunge into the heap of fallen leaves
and see the plane trees rise up above my head,
leafless, among the stars.

On happiness

The classics have spoken about it from their point of view,
so distant from ours. You can understand
Cicero and Montaigne, who are no help to you.
You have to look back farther, to know what's hidden
beneath the mask of myth,
that of ancient theatre,
the two holes for the eyes and that of the mouth.
That's what friendship is. Knowing
where the darkness comes from that is yours.

Power cuts

You had to climb on foot, groping your way
to the terrace roof with the broken lightning-conductor.
Being afraid made it even more humiliating.
The flat, open on all four sides, in front of the Pont de Pedra,
was a nest exposed to the open wings
of the vigilant vultures of innocence.
They are still there, perched on the rusted cable
from which the lightning-conductor used to hang.

At the top of the darkness of the stairs
there has always been this same shelter,
and in the other waves of light
my grandmother's eyes waited for me,
eyes worn out through so much watching
down roads along which no one ever returned.

At an exhibition

Everyone goes past this painting without stopping.
After the Rembrandts and the Dürers, I find myself
looking at a dog tied by a chain,
its shaggy fur marked by old beatings,
and keeping guard over nothing but the horizon.
Like a breeze which, blowing without stopping,
can rock an iron bridge and make it fall,
I sense that some humble force is stirring
feelings I have kept quiet about all my life.

This dog by Paulus Potter,
a seventeenth-century painter whom I didn't know,
is now part of an order and stands guard in my eyes.

Soviet music

Music is always a shortcut.
I listen to Shostakovitch
and my uncle's oily boilersuit comes to mind.
It sports La Maquinista's insignia.
I used to carry his lunch to him
in the train locomotive workshop.
Sitting beside him I kept him company
on that bit of waste ground with weeds and scrap metal.

He hoisted a Catalan flag
on top of the roof of La Maquinista.
The night the police came to the house
rumour had it some neighbours had denounced him.
A lie, for they were decent people,
but it took the folk at home many years
before they were able to believe they were innocent.
Having the same force as music,
calumny is another shortcut.
What to do with Shostakovitch?
With so much dissonance that it's a farewell?

'He hoisted a Catalan flag…': The Franco régime had outlawed any demonstration whatsoever of pro-Catalan feeling.

Birds and sacks

The throngs of sparrows sadden me
as they fly swiftly above the fields
and clamour with sharp, harsh cries
over that well-ploughed scarcity.
They have never ceased to keep me company.
It barely matters until the end.
Nor have I been abandoned by the smell of sacks
that made a bed for me at the bottom of the cart
when I went as a child to the grape harvest.
We left before daybreak. The jolting
of the wheels and the strong, steady rhythm
of the well-shod hooves lulled me to sleep.
The sacks still serve as a mother for me.
Their smell has returned, thick and warm,
while I see how the frost shines as the sun comes out
and the throngs of desperate sparrows
search for places where they may land
and sate a small, hard hunger.
They fly, they fly with me to the very end.

The house

Neoclassical, somewhat rationalist.
Its mouldings severe, discreet.
It has the strength of orderliness: I recognise
that firm resolve not to be exhibitionistic.
Builder and architect are now both dead.
I picture them, the building well-advanced,
observing it, perhaps from where I am now.
It's a good vantage point.
They will never know that today
we have once and for all kept death at bay.

The big parterre

My childhood died in Turó Park.
I can still see those summer mornings,
the brilliant greens and the happiness
with which we ran about, how we'd stop
at the little jets of those fountains
that I feel wetting my lips again.
The dazzle of light began in the lake
with the waterlilies' sumptuous whiteness
and the flight of dragonflies like angels
that would stop in one spot in mid-air.
And the light spread out, with the sparkling
of the water sprinklers, over the grass
of the big parterre: an open, forbidden space,
nothing but quiet grass, protected
by the border of white-painted stakes.
To my eyes, the calm of a huge garden.

Now they have removed the stakes and there is
a field of earth with patches of grass
because everyone walks their dogs there.
Freedom also reminds us
that we are the brutish people Pla spoke about.
And that it's easy to go back to being cruel.
That's what it means to remember: passing up
an opportunity for being happy.

Pla: Joseph Pla (1897-1981), a great Catalan writer.

Bad people and places of safety (1951)

The first great strike. People going to work
on foot, the trams empty.
Seeing the police arrive,
I didn't stop running until I was home.

My age has been one of ideologies,
but the idea is not intelligence.
Like the spark from the fire, the idea leaps
and is extinguished in the night.
An ideologue always carries inside him
an assassin, my father used to say
looking for a faction to save his life.

It snowed the following year.
The authorities, at college, covered up like the snow:
they complained gently but then froze hard.
I escaped to the white park,
at the limits of fear,
there where happiness begins.

Prince's Square

Santa Cruz de Tenerife

My romanticism doesn't begin
either with literature or with music,
but with the lowly hulls
of so many cargo vessels and so many mailboats
that made the trip between the islands.
It begins in the square, in the musicians' bandstand
beneath the rustling Indian laurels.

Life has assumed this shape
through the blazing of a mast with no flag.
The mailboats and cargo vessels will sail forever –
wrapped in oblivion, which is like nights at sea,
even though there are no stars –
rocked by the rough, warm waves,
all the way to Prince's Square.

Education

Precise and dangerous, poetry
will reveal to the boy and girl
the adolescent soul,
this sheet hung in a sinister street.
Poetry is the first logic.
It has always spoken of the same thing, and yet,
what it says is always new, just as the rising
of the sun or the sky at night is new.
Lost in the midst of their parents' failure,
will they find the strength that is capable
of seducing them with the truth?

The gramophone

It was a wooden piece of furniture, huge and dark,
polished like a mirror:
my father would never allow
anyone other than himself to work it.
He would always play the same record,
as though trying desperately
to find out why, when he listened to it,
it arrived somewhere.

Robert Schumann, *Concerto for piano*
played by Friedrich Gulda.
I go on listening to it and remember
a street of small houses in Las Palmas,
each with a goat on the flat roof.
In the background, the sea.

Military camp

Could a game like this, with fascinating moments –
the bugle call of 'lights out' on the parade ground –
be the same enthusiasm for killing?
Death was not present, as hundreds of well-
disciplined lads filed past, singing.
Until I closed my fist on a bullet
and my fist was a black heart. I couldn't know
at eighteen that reading Keats
was to read the orders of an armed horde.
That listening to Bach was to listen to a hundred hands
clashing guns at a single stroke.

J.A.G.H.

I picture you with a glass of rough wine
in the one-horse town from which you wrote me
that final letter. I say slowly:
I made a huge feint and lived twenty years.
The only line of yours that I remember
from those evenings at the Cafè de l'Òpera.
I always thought that, of us two,
it was you who'd be the poet, a skinny
Baudelaire from Extremadura.
My friend, missing for so long,
a voice on the telephone that from time to time
would surge up out of old hopes.
Suddenly I know that we two are now just one.
That it has stopped, the water wheel
of the fateful poem that you never finished writing.

Sant Jordi College

Everyone hid himself behind the signs
of that which would one day destroy him.
But how necessary, still, the years there,
when I read the nineteenth-century Russians:
from Chekhov and Tolstoy I learned
that salvation is self-knowledge.
Knowing the pain of words.
Freedom was already beginning to lose
its wager with fate, a fate that was like the blind
student who every night in the small hours
guided us through the darkness to raid the kitchen.

Light at Colera

Evening falls and, from the terrace,
listening to the leisurely waves,
I stare at the beach, with a lukewarm sun
and calm, green and orange sea before me.
I see a tall woman arrive,
almost naked, with a silent child,
and he is stark naked. They are the only ones on the beach.
The child sits down, and doesn't move.
The woman drops her gear and the clothes
and moves around him, picking things up
and dropping them again. She does not speak to the child.
All at once she leaves.
The child gets up and dips his feet in the sea.
He stands still looking at the horizon.
The woman comes back: she is carrying a drink.
I feel the chill of the setting sun on the nape of her neck.
She hasn't said a word to the child and they both stand
with their feet in the water.
The woman goes back and continues
her dance around her disorder.
Even distance cannot conceal the desolation.

The Museum of Modern Art

You reached it by walking through the park,
and in the museum there was never a soul.
The old radiators, the Nonell room:
those dark greens of his for poor women
huddled in shawls of gloom.
The shout of a red brush-stroke.

A custodian slowly crosses
the passage at the far end.
That museum loved me.
I could wish that a poem of mine
might be a room to succour someone.
The shout of a red brush-stroke.

Celebrity

He was one of the Catalans who won the war.
Once I found myself quite near to him
and he was shining with pride – it was in seventy-five –
in his fascist uniform:
blue shirt and white jacket
with the yoke and arrows and with the black belt.
When he died, the Government
honoured his corpse with a lying-in-state
at the Palau de la Generalitat.
Not a single member of Parliament opposed it.
I remember Xenophon: *The Retreat of the Ten Thousand*.
Abandoned by those who were leading them,
ignorant of the route and surrounded on all sides.
We have tried to survive and to make our way home.

The *Celebrity* of the poem is a prominent franquista politician who, when democracy was restored, made his career on the Olympic Committee and became the President of the International Olympic Committee. He cleaned up his image by awarding the Olympic Games to Barcelona in 1992. When he died, members of the Catalan Parliament were silent, and his corpse, as the poem tells, was given a lying-in-state at the Catalan Presidential Palace.

The angel's darkness

A night with no moon on a beach,
with boats round us and so young,
it was the serene radiance of your desire
that decided our life.
He was there, in the darkness, on the sand,
resonant in the nearby sound of the sea.
My fear and your confidence
were already aware how close the future
loomed, this angel who always
welcomes us in the deepest darkness.
Now it is here also, that night,
while you lie asleep beside me.
It is the same darkness: the angel's.

The dawns of the romantic man

I have never seen a flicker of anything that might
lead me to entertain great hopes,
but when the horizon stands clear-cut, backlit
by a sky already brightening,
I have always waited for a kind of meaning.

When, from a cargo ship, I have seen the sea awakening,
that there are thousands of years of literature.
Or else in the dawn breaking behind the sown furrows
that the order it illumines is the same
as that of lines of poetry and calculus.
Likewise when the dawn makes the back-
yard as sumptuous as a garden.
And above all in the dawn behind building sites:
that first construction when I saw
how my pride rose with it.

This clarity, that tends to last only a short time,
suddenly acquires its meaning:
I hope to be loved after my death.
Like the poor during the postwar years,
who waited in front of the slaughterhouse
for the bloody remains of animals' lights.
A mystical blue above the horizon.

Winter

When I turned fifty I bought myself
all eight volumes of Gibbon because I thought
that at the end of my life I would read them.
Sometimes I go over to where they stand,
and simply touching them with my hand calms me.
I haven't read them, but they keep me company.
Now, an imperceptible voice tells me
it's high time I started reading Gibbon:
Decline and Fall of the Roman Empire
is this History known as Universal,
the only kind that consoles.
As useless and magnificent as an aerial view.

Joan Maragall

The builders of old, in the outermost wall,
used to leave some ashlar blocks
protruding towards the neighbouring ground
so that, when building there, both houses
might remain firmly linked. Maragall
left these ashlar blocks in his work
so that we might attach our own to it.
With courteous, reasonable and
refined intelligence, he has shown me
that a good poem is always compassionate.
That compassion is essential
for a dignity
that no Catalan poet until now
has been able to attain as Maragall has.

Jacint Verdaguer (1845-1929) and Joan Maragall (1860-1911) were the first
modern Catalan poets.

Computing laboratory

Mornings with the rosy light that the first rays
of sun laid on the big windows.
An enormous computer dominated
with a lot of coloured lights blinking
desperately as it carried out calculations.
If my fate made of those years
a sad and difficult time,
how is it that I remember it as being so happy?
The truth frequently conceals itself
in some quite other feeling which is not
the one that reason is able to deduce.
The refuge of calculation and of calm
is still inside me. Its intimacy
blinks silently without ever stopping.
Desperately, in order to save my life.

A small church

Paris, Saint-Julien-le-Pauvre

No more than thirty people
are seated beneath the simple vault
of primitive Gothic. The rough stone
contrasts with the piano,
a Steinway, the programme tells us.

A Beethoven sonata begins,
number 27 in E minor,
severe as the walls.
The pianist is over fifty
and strikes the keys, attacking them,
avenging himself on a past that, inside the church,
resonates like the echo of a mistake.
The Gothic is understanding, and tolerates bitterness,
a snake that makes its nest in the depths of art.

Don't forget

I've never seen a gloomier hospital
than that old house with a garden
of a desolate green, grey with dusk.
We were with you: your mother
in your room at your bedside
and I in a small room with the doctor,
as though our stay was some other time
in a house and we the visitors.
Talking all night about medicine
and structural calculations, watching
a most slow and difficult moon
that, while it made you cruelly
grow pale, said to you: *stop playing now*.
Today, a long way off and sometimes
not knowing who there is who, truly,
weeps for you – dear daughter, don't forget.

Nothing exalts the old

Neither this violence in wanting
to be right. Nor believing that happiness
has anything, subtly, to do with lying.
Nor having as filthy a heart as those at home,
even though they were made filthy by the war.
My peace must be a bogus peace.
Nor failing to abjure lust
or vanity. How can it be that we go on
being vain, we the old? This is defeat.
On a battlefield where it has grown dark
the dead surround me and I can hear
the far-off voices of the young celebrating
what for them is still a victory.

Where the future ends

Will it never end, my daughter's
desolate and impossible future?
I remember the summers at S'Aucanada,
the sea shining and blue and pine trees
as strong as our hope.
Afterwards, the first winter: a storm
undermined the beach and dried up the great pines.
It was as though the coast of Mallorca,
ripping off its mask in rage,
were grieving over Joana's death.

First night at Forès

The house abandoned at the end of the war.
With the wind laying siege at the windows
and cries of night birds on the roof tiles,
it did not convey the peace of the fireside
in this world where you have to have a home.
Refuge lay in the stone walls.
The memories that were left were
the frozen soot varnishing the hearth.
To have a home you have to win the war.

Jazz

One night we took him with us
to his first concert.
He sat so quietly between you and me.
The light from the spots made an island of
piano and sax. In the dark, in his shy eyes,
there was the gleam of the instruments.
The most profound rightness of music
will be his shelter in the face of loneliness.
He will still have the warmth of his dead sister.
Our companionship. At any concert whatsoever.

Celebration

One night you went out, while I stayed with the children.
It started to snow and you came home late.
For the many years that we have lived on our own
I have risen early: it's snowing
just as on that night.
Without warning you, I get dressed, I leave the house,
I get the car out, I put on some music
and Bach roars out at highest volume on the piano
while the windscreen wiper sweeps
the snowflakes and I drive on to the motorway.
There is hardly any traffic. I sing at the top of my voice
this music that is impossible to sing.
An old man drives in the midst of the blizzard
through the night in pursuit of his love.

Poet

With my scissors for cutting
words like roses,
I had to search for gaps in time.
I found them in suburban bars
after visits to building works.
Gaps in time. I've ended up living there.
I see now, still standing, what remains of a wall.
In front of its dark structure,
that is unmasted, I have understood my life.

Summers at Campanet with Joana

Through porches whose doors
no one ever closed
you could see a courtyard
at the rear of every house:
courtyards with hydrangeas
in tin pots.

Black summer nights,
while there rang out
the melancholy clunking
of some goat-bell,
I heard a voice
warning me:
You will remember Mallorca
in every tear.

Its last door
is already closed.

Toast

Closer through that which no one will ever know,
we raise our two glasses.
We see our light, each in the eyes of the other.
A man and a woman, in an instant,
can be wrong.
But the instant will never come back.

Adultery

She has gone to bed with him and she's returning to work
with a feeling of relief, like when it stops raining.
In the bus she remembers the Book of Judith:
how the Bible, just like an archaic Freud,
puts a full-stop to that night of love.
But this Judith whom she is thinking about
and who carries a swathed head in her arms,
stops and looks behind her at the distant campfires
while she kisses those lips, that she finds still warm.
On the bus, the woman clutches
her handbag with the keys of home.

The badly-closed cage

It is years since he has recalled
those docile, gentle rabbits
that he found one morning decapitated.
A silence is coming,
a last mother's silence. The daughter, the child
who wept for the rabbits, does not speak.
Every word conceals another truth.
Like a badly-closed door.
The badly-closed door of forgetfulness.

Being who you say you are

You have built it all round yourself.
It has protected you and it has isolated you.
For the foundations built with admiration
beneath the walls of your poetry
you need feel no shame: they are secure.
They made the child suffer. But not the old man now.
You didn't think these walls would be so high.
Now, what you should worry about
is being who you say you are. There's nothing else
that might give you enough impetus to jump.

Fable

Tiny, like a lapdog, morality was a bitch,
one of those who never stop barking,
ugly as a rat. All day long sniffing around
and bothering the wolf-dog of life
which, impassive and strong, never even glanced her way.
Today I saw him go past into the garden
with morality gripped between his jaws,
caught by the scruff of her neck, afraid and cringeing.
She was not barking, she was now emitting
piercing, hair-raising yelps,
but life, with the wolf's firm step,
carried her in amongst trees full of birds,
broke her spine and afterwards
went to lie in the shade.
Today I have made a clearance of my books,
the ones of my own time, I mean.
Those by Simone de Beauvoir I have thrown out, all of them.

Poem of the last refuge

Before, I used to concentrate while I listened
to my thought in the midst of every kind of din.
Nowadays it is so hard to do it.
I am not tired of life: I am tired
of the voices that blare emptily around me.
But I know where happiness still goes on:
If I have never lost any paradise,
I'll not lose the most austere of all,
the one where the poem retains
barely a trace of literature.
I recognise this place, I have searched for it always.
The last refuge, that of solitude.

The goodbye

He underlined as he read: he did it as though the book
were a house on fire.
His mind was searching for something
implacable and abstract that they had hidden from him.
Lots of pages ended up covered
by underlinings in pencil and ink,
black and coloured, one on top of another.
His meticulous, confused self-portrait.

His face gradually set
in the fixed expression of an anger
that came from having lost his way
in some profound incompetence.

And later there arose
the innocent smile of his silence.
He didn't know me:
I was part of the lands
he had with such effort won back from the sea
and which the sea was flooding again.

Summer night

We always washed up the dishes, she and I, together,
right here, facing the window
which, above the kitchen sink, opens on to the sea.
A long way off and all by itself there is a house
at the top of a cliff, and I do not remember
ever having seen any light shining there.
For years I have washed up alone. I'm doing it now,
after supper, the window open wide
on a warm and moonless night.
I listen to the waves breaking like time:
they are the restlessness of the sea far out.
Suddenly, I raise my eyes to the darkness,
I stop what I was doing, hands in the water:
where the house stands, there's a window with a light on.

Altamira

I have forgotten life. Together, all my memories
would not last longer than a few hours.
They are like my ashes:
from them are made the ochres and rusty reds
in order to paint these poems in the cave
of consciousness: my shelter,
as lonely and dark as Altamira.

Having coffee as day is breaking

In the midst of the traffic's noisy anxiety
life can glide along smoothly
calm and distant, in some bar or other.
A smile lurks in a corner near the big window:
it is neither inside nor out, it is simply absence.
Each of us rocks an empty cradle
and looks away,
towards the spot where childhood's
red, peremptory sun rises.

White clouds in the blue air

It is sometimes as clear as this, my memory.
Your not being is as luminous as you,
which is why I have looked for no further consolation
than to keep hold of the thread of your smile.
So as not to lose you, I have not to clench
my fist as tightly as at your death.
But it will happen.
It will be when, on a day of wild wind,
I let go the thread of your kite, Joana.

Being from there, going there

Gazing at my grandparents' faces was like following the trail
of a wounded fugitive who hides himself in history.
There remained shame, not rage,
buried as they buried the mules
and the dogs in the ploughland.
And, in spite of everything, our language. Gnawed at
beside the fire in the hearth by the withered faces
that were mistrustful, but wearing a slight smile
of peasant irony. And, in spite of everything,
windows. Humble and generous
in the light joined to silence.
The fire has not gone out. The language sings.
As for the windows,
I have always lived close to their panes of glass.
They are the only cold that protects me from the cold.

Goodbye, Tel-Aviv

I cross the hallway of the small hotel,
where the taxi driver is waiting, and the night porter.
I go out into the dark of early morning.
Goodbye, streets of Tel-Aviv,
so lonely at this hour:
the dignified, rationalist clarity,
the only force for becoming a people,
for grasping and throwing away all the keys
of the houses from which you were driven out.
The taxi gathers speed, and the Moroccan
Jew searches for music on the radio.
I search for words for this farewell,
words that may sink into the soil
and rot slowly there like leaves
towards a spring that is bound to come.
Goodbye, streets of Tel-Aviv:
this morning early, while I feel
someone placing a humble stone
of farewell upon my tomb,
your hard freedom comes with me.

Making a source ripple

The lack of hope in my people
is a lack of hope in me.
I've got the mists of France in my eyes.
I have a melancholy affection for the rivers of forgetting
and the barges full of shadow that sail along them.
Three centuries of failures separate me
from Villon's lines, which I no longer understand.

Infidelity

My solitude pushed you into it.
Little by little everything runs towards guilt,
which is the hardest form of love.
Prints from when we stumbled,
as though into fresh, glistening cement,
there where no one should have trod.
I still attempt to embed my feet there
in pointless solidarity.
Aeschylus and Sophocles showed us
that it is in guilt that we let go of life.
I will not forget your cry, which I never heard.
It is the voice of my solitude.

Fifty years later

The cold, dark, transparent air
flows beside and supports the aluminium wings
of the night flight coming into Santa Cruz.
The descent begins above the embers
void of warmth of a brightly-lit city
that long ago concealed the poor, lost lamps
of my adolescent dream.
My Atlantic was warm waters
and the lava sand of the beaches.
Nights meant streets with few street lights
where the asphalt was alive with cockroaches,
where the volcano rose, alone and surrounded by stars.
To suppose that the laurels,
when the breeze passes over them,
would always be there, searching for me,
is the prodigal son's mistake. Returning
never fails to wipe out any trace of happiness.

When everything was simple

The war had carried off the furniture
from the house let out in a cowed
and suspicious Sant Gervasi. The garden
was a piece of ground full of brambles and nettles
but still held its rose bush.
My mother was forever telling me that a rose
perfumes the hands of the one who plucks it.
Nowadays there remain few with any scent.
What have we gained, then? Freedom.
My freedom for a rose
like Rilke's or Juan Ramón's.

Towards dusk

My father walks very upright, hands clasped behind his back
and, at his side, my mother
carries my sister in her arms.
Joana hurries after with her crutches,
she doesn't want to be left behind.
I can barely make out my grandparents, far off.
My mother says: *Let's go, it's getting late.*
We are getting closer to the second death,
they are ever fewer, those who remember us.
They all walk quickly, the sun sets,
they are going, they are leaving me, and Joana's
soft voice says: *goodbye, Daddy.*
Now it's hard to hear them in the mist.
And the last word, the deepest,
echoes, lonely and heavily, in my head.

The beginnings of something

Sometimes your eyes take on once more
the abstract, sensual gaze of the hunter.
Whom do you desire if no woman wants
an old man to caress her, not even with his eyes?
There remains dignity, that wolf-dog
which, lying beside you, no one sees.
It slips through twilight's windows,
where your gaze frays a path
through the evergreen cypresses while you feel
a happiness that, when you were younger,
you would never have dared even imagine.
You will never overturn the course of anything.
Your absence will soon be
as logical as the lights are now
that have come on along the horizon.

Song of gratitude

Never have I felt the kind of enthusiasm
that Mayakovsky or Whitman felt. To feel it
you have to fire off hopes into the future.
Ithaca does not dazzle me. I doubt whether any journey
could be anything that the traveller was not
before setting out. That is why
I carry the *Iliad* in my heart, rather than the *Odyssey*.
I have been a practical man.
Abrupt, faithful, solitary. Grateful.

A sentimental tale from memory

Love and time are a conflict
that always resolves itself through pain and forgetting.
Because understanding does not mean loving,
but rather distancing oneself further: this I suspected
years ago in fact, when I was still an architect.
I have to re-learn everything.
All I need now is the loyalty
to something vague and solitary,
as hard as a rock in the middle of the sea.
Sometimes an older person's mind
furiously sets its logic in motion.
Look how it wanders through its memories:
it travels along a desolate coast,
because understanding does not mean loving,
but rather distancing oneself further: I have to re-learn everything.

Visits to building works

For many years I began my day
amid the ordered disorder of building works.
There is one starting in front of the house.
I often contemplate it,
I remember how day would gradually break
in the midst of the screeching
of discs as they cut out steel planks,
and the outrageous din of the pile-driver.
Piercing and breaking in order to build:
this contemporary music
of justified destruction.

After my visit
I'd look for a bar where I could be alone, safe
from the din, but inside the din,
with the grey angel of the structure in the windows.
The concrete sky in the suburbs,
damp, always hardening, all the iron
rusted, industrial, a tenderness
I still feel when time throws hailstones
against the glass of my private life.
Life ends the way building sites begin:
piercing and breaking in order to build.
A justified destruction.

THIRD BOOK

From Where to Begin to Love Again

(2014)

Love is a place

From my seat on the train I gaze at the landscape
and suddenly, fleetingly, a vineyard goes by
which is the lightning-flash of some truth.
It would be a mistake to alight from the train
because then the vineyard would vanish.
Love is a place, and there is always something
that reveals it to me: a distant field,
a conductor's empty stand with only a rose on it,
and the musicians playing on their own.
Your room as day was breaking.
And, of course, the singing of those birds
in the cemetery, one morning in June.
Love is a place.
It endures beyond everything: from there we come.
And it's the place where life remains.

Autumn friendship

They have grown so tall, the trees in the garden,
that they give us the measure of the past.
Of how I no longer understand it, from such a distance.
Of how nice it is, from so far away,
to wait for someone who will never come back.
The tallest poplar has dropped
its mound of leaves that have gone on covering the lawn.
Every year we have patiently swept them up.
Now that the bare branches let it through,
the sun silently
enters the room and shines on the floor.
Only the wind disturbs the heap of fallen leaves,
or the wild boars, some morning or other.
This year we shan't sweep up the leaves.
We're consoled by the golden reflections of a disorder
that goes deep into the grave understanding of winter.

The failure

The scene is a bedroom
into which, like an underlying pain,
there flows the light from the street.
There is a woman sleeping: her clothes,
laid out neatly upon a chair,
are one of the characters. The other
is a man gazing at the black knickers.
In his eyes his conscience
is reflected, a volcano into which,
sooner or later, he will end up throwing himself.
He leans over the crater, but it's too dark.
He stares at the black knickers like a wolf
staring at prey that is out of its reach.

Aubade

It is not yet day.
They leave the nest and sing.
The ones belonging to guilt do so
while hidden and a long way off.
Those with the clearer voice
are the ones belonging to sadness.
Those that belong to solitude,
that sing for love,
do not sing for anyone.
Strong, close by, can be heard
the song of those who are not there.

I come from there

I live in cities with high buildings,
inclined, skewed, which exhibit
ostentatiously the power of danger
and of folly.
Titanium and glass reflecting the clouds.
But life too is scaffolding,
humble skeletons for climbing up.
Like a Shakespearean villain, opulence
is always plotting a crime.
And I am a letter, badly-written
by those who opened a way for water to reach the orchards.
I come from there. Whatever nobility there may be in me
cannot come from anywhere but poverty.
That which humbly removes the scaffolding
from straight-built, perpendicular, traditional walls.
The poverty that with the hoe broke up the soil.
I have known it. I know what it is.
I shall never confuse it with all that other,
all that is mean in opulence.

Helping

As twilight begins,
I gaze at the coombed ceiling under the tiled roof:
crooked beams that once were trees,
one lying beside another, varnished,
bearing the weight of the roof
and the snow that has fallen all afternoon.
They will withstand the weight of this night,
and maybe I will be the one who from time
to time withstands from inside a poem
so that a woman, in her troubled night,
may say of me: how he bears this insomnia,
the grief, the snowfall of my eyes.

Barcelona

This name is still a place to shelter in.
The civil sanctity of greed
and also the generous rebuff
of the dead on Montjuïc, facing the sea.
Where is that cultured middle class?
And those workmen who, as well as their trade,
knew poems by heart?
What can still bind me to a city
whose face I see with its make-up
like that of a dead mother?
In silence, I listen to the iron of the trams
that passed, when I was young, along the Rambla:
a sonata of poverty and roses.
But in Montjuïc I have two daughters,
and now I find offensive a strange crowd,
who are dazzled by the pointless glitz
of icy hotels and superfluous shop windows.
It's usually in shelters
that it's colder, at times, than anywhere else,
you desolate city going a-whoring.

Montjuïc: the steep hill with the cemetery of Barcelona. It faces the sea.

A woman of sense

You're ironing clothes and I'm putting them away
while we listen to the husky voice
of Edith Piaf singing *Je ne regrette rien*.
You begin on the shirt and stop:
the collar is worn.
'It's too old,' you say. 'We'll turn it into dusters.'
You pick up the scissors and cut it up,
and I turn off the music
because that hoarse voice and the violins,
I realise, are nothing more than skeletons
dressed in rags, executing a grotesque dance.
My fears are thirty years ago.
For us too the past –
and this you already knew – is coming to an end.

Arcadi Volodos: sonata D.984

This music is modest
like supper in the kitchen, hospitable
like having had children, and it takes pity
on this body which the tide
drags to the wintry beach of each of us.
What frankness in the most abrupt notes
telling me: what seems hostile, that too is love.
As the piano's reverberation dies away,
what I have heard goes on making me tremble.
Schubert's music
is a form of loving-kindness

Grief

Night returns.
Hunger is over now.
Latin and mistrust are over.
Over, too, the breaking day of geography,
freedom in the woods.
The crossings are over, too,
to a distant island.
Green and black gazing at an ocean.
You have come,
the loyalty of happiness.
The noises of building works.
The sensible disorder of her death.
Night returns. The moon.
Night returns.
Night
always
returns.

Pillage

When I was a child they wanted to pluck out the tongue
that my grandmother spoke to me in
as we came home from the fields at the end of the day.
Like stones, flowers, loneliness,
all around, keeping us company, are words.
Mutilated and all,
they have ended up saying what they had to say.
Caught on brambles, there must still be
that closed Lleidan *é* that I lost.
Having saved my tongue has left me
at the mercy of a people that were mine.

A generous time

Ours, like the songs that make us cry,
those days are.
They were the truth of when it grew dark
with smiles, bathing the children.
The happy weariness of supper.
The faces that have no longer
turned to us as then, confidingly.
Life is fed by generous days.
By giving and protecting.
When you have been able to give, death alters.

Distant

A stray dog goes down the road
looking for slavery in danger.
Panting, as evening draws in, he still has the strength
to bark at the first headlights, that dazzle him.
The road lies beside the sea
on a steep bit of coast.
The world may be utterly beautiful
but it must include humiliation.
Dreaming is nothing more than looking for a master.

Mother and son

The woman walks a few steps ahead,
and she nails a single thought to the air.
Behind her the child is talking to himself,
stops, hops a bit, sings in a low voice.
She doesn't see him. How can she know that he's there?
That the child isn't far away? Indeed, that he won't come back?
We should forget childhood,
forget the silence that always preceded us.
That still precedes us in certain places.
Life is sinking into vulgarity
and into mere illusion. Into vulgarity
for having risked it so little at the beginning.
Into mere illusion for risking it
in desperation when the end comes.

The silent man

He was a clever poet
who, though he was dealt poor cards,
knew how to play them
and write the poems that he wrote.
Passing the house where he used to live, I recall
the staircase with its landing that he sang of.
It always moves me to understand
why he never composed certain poems.
It's where the ones I wrote began.
Poetry is what follows on
from something that has never been.
I stare at myself in Joan Vinyoli's mirror
and I know how he went about
finding a place from where to begin to love again.

Joan Vinyoli: Catalan poet (1914-1984).

Greeting

With the years you have learned this gesture quite well.
You meet the neighbour and you greet each other,
side by side, two old men on the pavement,
each one closing his front door.
Houses, then. The generous exchange
of a few words in the street.
Beyond this there can be nothing more,
or else it's the final passion, the calm
when you remember fierce, lonely memories
beneath a patch of sky, clean as a sum.
Each in his own backyard
turning, little by little, into a door.
It opens every morning. Every evening it closes.

Days in Turó-Park, 1948

The tall red-brick block of flats,
on to whose back my house looked out,
received a lot of light: it opened on to the nastiness
of building lots in the outskirts and suburbs.
In front was the park with its orderliness
of dark, mysterious, urban green.
The waste ground at the back,
with too much light, always frightened me.
Like an allegory of the devastated
country where I was born. As for the front,
I was frightened of ending up feeling an intruder
in a really beautiful park, never having been
an upper-class English romantic.
Splendour and grime make for poor symmetry.
I like to go back to the park from time to time.
There I discovered that in order to be free
those who love you must not know where you are.

Man walking above a sea of mist
(Caspar David Friedrich, 1818)

I put myself in his place and feel the chill
of all I am turning my back on.
Socrates' words are a farewell.
Far from its classics and helpless,
intelligence needs, as vultures do, the flesh of dead animals.
Life is not sentimental,
not one of its laws is compassionate:
out of the fear this produces I have spoken love,
at once the cunning of a slave
or that kind of faithfulness
which, for an old man, is knowledge.
I need the vulture's sight
to see what isn't there.
Behind me where I stand on a rock I feel
that cold Socratic breath on the back of my neck.

Self defence

There are few books that can still dazzle me,
and little music left to me that might console.
It's the rats of time. They leave nothing.
I do what I can to keep bright
all the humble gold I've saved up till now.
That's why I talk to those who aren't there
and I always smile as I do so, and never go
where death is business, and the flowers ugly.
Knowing how to be sad is a strength.
The last one to be lost. Beyond this point
there are very few books and very little music
capable of resisting an enthusiasm
which is of the animal and of poverty.

Republican ghost on the Rambla

(Ferran La Rosa)

Good morning, commander. You saved
my father from being shot
and together you raised a glass to me while already
the corpse of a nation was floating down the Ebro.
I would never have been able to put a face to you
among the crowd, but you strolled,
like them, beneath the plane trees of the Rambla,
with war's cape and pistol,
trying to make your way
as far as the sea, stretched
like a taut sheet on the line of the horizon.
Look: it's nothing but scenery.
There is nothing behind the façades.
Or just our quarrels, commander.
Thank you for saving us. Now, go your way
with the only soldiers at your disposal:
your name spoken by me, the wind in the plane trees.
Let the river of people carry you away,
a murmurous Ebro that goes on
dragging that same corpse away.

'the corpse of the nation…': The last great battle of Spanish Civil War, on the
banks of the Ebro.

One of so many lost tragedies

Childhood learned never to ask questions.
To stare at the family's dark corner.
And when the old were now dead
the questions returned, full of anguish.
But they were too late:
there would never be any answers. The dead
would stay all by themselves in those years
and I in mine.

There are still remains of bunkers and shelters.
The invisible rights
of what they called freedom.
I think I held in my hands
the original of a classical tragedy
that I've never been able recognise.

Like a Rembrandt

On one side, the fields,
the dark places crossed by wild boar and fox.
On the other the flagstones of the courtyard, glazed
by the sheaf of golden light that pours from the doorway.
Like an expulsion
that has the force of a welcome.
Our very last door. I recover
the old impulse, the ray of light
in the darkness from where to begin to love again.

Fog

Nothing so humble has ever
kept me such company
turning my winter
mornings into a refuge.
Nor had anyone looked at me
from a window
with such patience.
As though there were someone
at the glass taking care of me.
No more going out. Where to?

Rainy afternoon in the courtyard

Now that I'm like an old spade,
rusted and still digging up soil,
could you recognise in me that young father?
Darkness, Joana. I'm making my peace with the dark
because, since you are there, it too is home.
Sitting in the shelter of the porch
I talk to you, listening to the rain falling.
Beneath the flashes of lightning, hearing the cordial
and cavernous voice of the storm,
we come out, from two different places, into the courtyard.
The Universe, without any religion,
which swallows us and spits us out is here as well,
where smooth, bluish aspidistras
envelop a classical bust made of marble
brought from a garden that was sacked during the war.
In the humble sound the rain makes as it falls
there is the far-off origin of words.
If you could see me, an old man now, listen again
to those birds singing around the coffin in flower.
If you could see me, Joana, lean over into absence
just as when as a child, finding a well,
I would always lean over
to call to the bottom of the water.
We talk in the quiet greenness of the ivy
that trembles with your name in the rain,
Joana, turned into my song.

City

Stopped at a traffic light, you smile at me
with the evening sky filling the windscreen.
It seems that this ending of ours
is like that of the *Alexandria Quartet*,
when she is caught, trapped underwater,
and he saves her by severing one of her hands.
Mutilating for love.
I too smile back at you, remembering
what in all innocence
I claimed when in my youth:
that my poems would never be literature.

Calm

Day closes, the roadside birds are silent
and the gale of time no longer stirs the leaves.
I shall try to cross these final years
in winter boots, in an intimacy
that's wrapped up warm like feeble feet.
I do not forget that I've never lacked
a kitchen in which to shelter.
The orderliness of clean windows.
I hear in my head the murmur of a torrent
that never sleeps.
I go further off so that in the darkness
I may see the stars more clearly,
scattered and shining flames.
Even with little strength I shall be able
to blow them out and make a wish:
if I'm not to come back,
may the snow fall on the path to the house.

The last time

(to the memory of Javier de Cambra)

I listen to a sax while rain falls
and I remember his humour and friendship.
Intelligent and disappointed,
ruined by the bad life
of those who persisted in believing
that Spain as a country was anti-Franco.
We called him The Theoretician.
I'm talking about the *Paraula de Jazz* years.
Sax, piano, bass and two poets.
But he was the one who knew most about jazz.
A bar where one of the piano keys
didn't sound, a suburban night club
and, finally, a quiet *Modernista* theatre.
We could have been two good friends.
We said goodbye not knowing
that between him and me there would be nothing but
the bad news and a poem.

Lovers on the metro

The journey rocks them both from side to side:
obese, roughly in their fifties, their clothes
sad with being so much pulled on and taken off.
Inside the tunnel their indigence is more marked,
as is a boozy unease, an expression
that's just beginning to verge on the witless.
She has begun giving him kisses
and to caress him awkwardly
while murmurung into his ear.
They both keep smiling, showing teeth
as higgledy-piggledy as birds at dawn.
The train pulls in to where they alight: with a sharp
exhalation, the doors have closed behind them
and now no one smiles, and the jolts
mark the rhythm of minds like wolves
searching for where to begin to love again.

Deluded

Now that I know it to be barren and harsh,
life is kinder to me.
The mistake was a romantic one:
thinking that enthusiasm and conviction
could bear it all.
Above a rock there is still a poetic sky
that I look at sideways. It has never protected me.
I have been deluded, but I'm no coward.
Dreaming has compelled me
to learn to read and write in the dark.
That has made me stay alert –
like a whore's difficult client –
to the slightest murmur of love.

On the ground

Like those ships that used to anchor,
laden with silks, in Venice,
the final solitude comes to me from far away.
It brings me fresh strength to confront despondency
over the meaning of life, so difficult
to discover because it's irrelevant.
The fault is mine if the sacred
has become grotesque.
The skeleton with the scythe that Dürer engraved
is now of no use: today he would have to engrave
a brightly-lit window in a dark street.

Contemporary music

Hosokawa, Ligeti, Gubaidulina, Henze, Schnittke

The Requiems composed for my time
are as though they mixed gregorian chant
with the violent, untimely sounds
of a building under construction.
In them can be heard the murmur of the future.

They are the rage and terror at our world.
Perhaps, too, a warning
for the orphanhood that remains in those places
that were lit up until a while ago by one of the classics.
Whoever thinks that our music is gross, even loathsome,
is bound to be wrong in not realising
that another Orpheus is now being born and singing
with the deafening cries of the newborn.

Knowledge

Digging among the stones, the clods of earth
and the roots you'll never pull out.
But this is the cost of what lies deep.
Digging is a religious act.
It's a form of goodness.
Digging at night. And then kneeling
and lifting your eyes to the stars
knowing you have to search for everything in the ground:
how to build a house, how to write a poem.
And even the place from where to begin loving again
in this tempest of memory.

Hunger

I was climbing the steps holding up a loaf of bread
that I have always remembered
as bigger and more luminous than it should have been.
And once indoors I cut it into slices.
Some days later, everything went back
to how it used to be, but the myth
had already begun to protect me.
I felt my own time, which was already another,
like a wind in my face.
A war that for the grown-ups would never end
came to an end for me in that moment.

José Emilio Pacheco's wheelchair

I'm walking beside the chair
that somebody else is pushing, clumsily.
Mexico. As we come out of the hotel together, the wheel gets stuck.
See how I kneel down, Joana,
to release the footrest
and set his legs comfortably in place?
All my life with you has suddenly come back,
and I don't want to get up because it's you
that I'm helping.
See how I manoeuvre as we go up the step?
Do you remember how I used to push you
in your chair and you rolled along happily?

I began this poem in the present.
The news reaches me in Barcelona.
He is, already, with Joana.
Now two empty wheelchairs
keep each other company
while, on both sides of the Atlantic,
a windy and unforgetting present
strikes every day with less and less rhetoric.

Aguascalientes, with Cristina and José Emilio, 9 November 2013.
Sant Just, 16 February 2014.

November journey

The storm breaks
as he leaves the hotel,
alone in a city
that she showed him.
Through the downpour, he barely
manages to make out
way up high the lights
of the Chrysler Building.
To love is to correct,
suppress, qualify.
To search for what to rescue
and from which place.
A wind is lashing
his face with branches of rain.
Don't go back on your own,
a desolate man mutters,
who learns furiously now
from where to begin to love again.

Babel

I dreamed that I had to make the calculations
for a building of a thousand floors
and there was no foundation
capable of supporting it.
I felt the vertigo that comes
from placing all one's hopes up high.
I awoke and, waiting for dawn,
I am shaken by that other vertigo that is greater,
because I know that each will forget the other
in eternity. Then
I went back to the heights, a dream
where we wanted to save what we loved.
We never could do it. Calculations don't lie.
No foundation
could support so much hospitality.
Neither of iron nor of love.

Hotel Colón, Barcelona

Cela was lying naked in the bath
and, wearing a sports jacket, I was sitting
on the lid of the lavatory arguing
that *Mrs Caldwell speaks to her son*
was his best book.
Towards evening, the Colón switched on all the lights
in front of the dark and fake
cement façade of the Gothic cathedral.
An enormous lie.
A complicated shame.
I hear Cela's booming, pompous voice
admonishing me from a sordid place
devoid of homeland where the order given is
the single line of an inhospitable law
that is always just:
love your own time, a dubious place
– but the only one that is yours –
where *Mrs Caldwell speaks to her son.*

Mrs Caldwell speaks to her son: In this stream-of-consciousness novel by Camilo José Cela, the widely translated Nobel Prizewinner, a woman is speaking to her dead son.

Your dead one

I *Train in the night*

With no lights
it is coming to a halt
in the middle of a wood,
where not even
a distant bark
breaks the darkness.
In one carriage
there is still a window
that is faintly red,
but which is just
darkening.
And, behind it,
the blurred, beloved
silhouette
of – even now – somebody.

II *It is getting light*

Held high and in the sun, my head goes
to another place where the watchful birds
have fallen silent and, like a train,
I have been halted by the snowstorm.
I am quiet in the wood, where I have returned
to talk to you, and I say nothing. Slowly
the birds start coming back. And it's this
that I wanted to tell you: I shan't move
but don't let it worry you. It means I love you.

Golden wedding anniversary

Woman who with a white-haired passion
make time fall in love,
retaining your cold fastidiousness
of winter blue.
Love is now this intelligence
of an erotic and kindly glance
that no longer needs to lie.

Out of the north courtyard that ends up being life,
you have made this garden.
My intimate Venus,
silent sensuality
of the strength our memory has.
Only sex warms.
There are tears that are the best protected.
Wolves and vultures guard them.

The poem

Lying on the table there is a small notebook.
Before going to bed, you glance at the last page.
With alterations, difficult to read, it shows words scored out.
And others, new ones, in the margins.
Dashes crossing the paper
to move a line from one place to another.
Going over it once again, you stop as you read:
These poems are searching for where to begin to love again.
You go to the window:
the street is empty.
And you go back to the table,
where the poem continues.
It's here, with you.

False alarm

(Erich Maria Remarque: Arc de Triomphe*)*

In the middle of the night
a false alarm has gone off.
Sleepy and half-dressed, we the guests
make our way down the stairs to the snowy street.
Nobody speaks. We are cold.
We resemble my heroes,
the ones from those novels by Remarque:
they lived under a false name in sordid hotels
and a past in ruins.
We are my sordid heroes,
I say to myself
while I listen to the guests' faceless silence.
Behind us, the future like the hotel in darkness.
There are no false alarms. They are all true.

Identity

What to do with words in the end?
If I want to discover what I am I can't search
anywhere but two places: childhood and the now of old age.
It's where my night is clean and cold
as the principles of logic. The rest of life
is the confusion of all that I've not understood,
Tedious uncertainties over sex,
useless flashes of intelligence.
I cohabit with sadness and happiness,
implacable neighbours. My truth
now approaches, hardest and plain.
Like those trains from when I was a child,
playing on the platforms, that passed right beside me.

Epilogue

IT WAS NOT FAR-OFF OR DIFFICULT. It is here now, this time which is not mine, in which I live in a bittersweet mix of proximity and distance. I feel how strange everything around me is becoming. Already I no longer recognise some values and modes of behaviour that today are commonplace. Landscapes are changing too quickly. No, this time is not mine, but it is now, in large measure thanks to poetry, that I feel some gusts of calm happiness that years ago I never knew.

It was not far-off, this age in which nobody hesitates to think of me as old, though always with some precautions that make me smile, since they are due to the absurdly bad press that this word receives, especially when it is followed by the noun, man. Nor was it difficult to come to a natural, even pleasurable understanding of some feelings from which the young make great efforts to distance or defend themselves. Solitude and sadness, for example. I think that the acceptance of these feelings is a kind of clockwork mechanism that life sets about activating in order to place death on a familiar horizon. I have understood the most dangerous replies that the proximity of death may generate and which are to be found between two extremes: despair and headlong flight, that is to say, submission to the values of youth. And thus, too, a kind of desperation. Equidistant, there is lucidity, the step before dignity. And wonder, the threshold of love, as the alternative to resentment and scorn.

These last few years, I have realised that, while the capacity for learning dwindles, there arises, as counterpoint, another capacity which will end up being the most important: that of utilising, in order to explore new intellectual and sentimental territories, everything that has been learned in life up until now. In this way one can achieve the lucidity necessary for understanding fear. But this new capacity depends on how the development of the inner life has been achieved. There is no way of avoiding a certain irreversibility of the situation. That is what determines whether this final stretch may be the most profound, but also the most banal of someone's life.

Fear is nothing more than the lack of love, a pit we try to fill – futilely – with a huge variety of things, acting directly, with no subtleties, a never-ending task, for the pit remains as empty and dark as ever. When you don't understand fear, all you can attempt is this un-nuanced action, which is that of selfishness, because it can take account only of filling one's own emptiness, without knowing whence it comes. At this point, love is perhaps not far-off, but it is difficult. You have to go back to the time before the pit, and know when and how it began to open up. At my age that is ineluctable. The substitution of fear by lucidity is what I call 'dignity'. It is then that it turns out that love was neither far-off nor difficult.

The word 'dignity' comes from the Latin dignus, 'worthy', and this meaning evolves into the more complex ones of 'worthy of respect' and, more importantly, that of 'self-respect', which is the meaning that interests me. This dignity which is respect for one-self leads towards love, which penetrates at the same time through intelligence, feeling and sensuality, which occurs inside each one of us and which is only circumstantially to do with public activities dedicated to the most needy, actions which belong, whether implicitly or explicitly, to the realm of politics.

Loving is complex enough to need all the tools and skills we acquired during our apprenticeship. I have found no better way of loving others than through the practice of poetry, sometimes as reader and other times as poet – I have stated more than once that for me the two options are one and the same – and putting, whether composing or interpreting a poem, the same honesty that I would desire and attempt to practise in any aspect of public or private life. I think that this exposition is possible because poetry has the intensity of truth.

Whatever a poet is, that will his poems be also: and there is no one harder to deceive than good readers of poetry. In the long run, a person of culture is someone who can tell Xuang Tsé from a guru of famous singers, a work by Montaigne from a self-help book. There is not a single good poem in which its author has not implicated himself or herself in some way right the way through. It is this that makes of it an act of love. 'somebody loves us all', as the wonderful final line of 'Filling Station', by Elizabeth Bishop, says.

In the midst of all this, the kind of poetry that most continues to interest me moves in a territory that I would call prudent, avoiding, in its relationship with the mysterious, the two extremes towards which the fallacy of originality is always attempting to push it. On one hand, there is the devaluation of the mysterious, which has already converted one part of the contemporary plastic arts and music into something that is alien to risk and emotion, and therefore to truth. The other extreme consists in emphasising it in an exaggerated way, that is to say, in ignoring the fact that even the mysterious, or especially the mysterious, ought to be treated sensibly. That the meaning or explanation of something may be unknown does not imply that any explanation whatsoever may be acceptable, however outlandish it may be. In spite of its exactness and concision, poetry can never be a short cut.

My own time has fled and left me alone in another time but my solitude is a luxurious one. It makes me think of Machiavelli's final exile in the rural world of his childhood, of those inns where, as he relates in his memoirs, he talked only to rough, uncultured peasants. But when night came he set a great table with the best and finest cloths, vessels and glasses, which he had brought from Florence, and he supped and talked with the wise men of Antiquity.

As for me, in this other exile which is, by its very nature, the final stage – long or short – of life, I feel that I myself am my own interlocutor. I do not now have time to improvise, I should have already spoken, long since, with the wise men of ancient times or of now, so that, through my poems, I might find myself with myself in the territory of dignity. The dignity of not being afraid of my fate.

But there comes a day when the past demands order and, thus, special attention for the mysterious question of memories. Because past and future disappear at the same time, as if by some law of physics, and more and more I have the feeling that the mind has not kept random fragments but rather the essence of the past. That is, what we remember, albeit not true, is, however, the truth. And truth – and I think this is what Josep Pla means when he speaks of poetry and biographies – is the deep aim of poetry. Therefore, the poetry that one has read, just like the music that one has listened to, are some of the elements, and probably not the least important ones, that intervene in the making of this essence.

Because poetry is a tool to manage pain and happiness, especially in their most domestic aspects, sadness and joy, the management of which depends on what is saved from the past. This essence is the subject of the poems in this book. As I was writing them, verses would emerge around a memory, which would fight with strength to get hold of the poem. Then I had to return it harshly to the exact role that it had to play, because what the memory wants to explain when it appears is still very far from the truth.

I feel that I come from a time marked above all by the fear at the end of the civil war, by the silence of executions and of prisons with which the victors exerted their vengeance. With the elders in the house taking care that I wouldn't be cold or hungry. That is where my Houses of Mercy come from. The ultimate meaning of every poem. But I realise that in order to understand a memory I must be able to connect beginnings and endings, that in order to understand what my grandmother represented for the beginning of my life I had to be able to compare it with what the life of my daughter Joana, as well as her death, represented much later in my life. I need to connect the time during which I wrote my last books of poems with the time that I spent alone with my mother in that village where she was a teacher.

And I also have to link my current idea of what poetry is with the teacher who taught me to write without grammar, directly. It took me years to distinguish a preposition from an adverb, but from the first moment he taught me to write correctly. The poet that I am has lived off this. Of course he taught us all this in Spanish, because I never heard Catalan at school. This repression carried out by means of the amputation of speech is one of the most durable and cruelest ones. I know now that I will die with this fear and this fragility surrounding the perception of my tongue, which means, also, of my life.

Something cries out in our first memories. Their austere clarity, like a bird's first flight. They are the only primal thing that we have left. A fierce joy despite having been born amid the horror of a murderer's country. The child knew what the old man can confirm now: that we must know how to use loneliness as a way of dealing with pain and misfortune, and with the cruelty with which this country has always imposed oblivion. All this is now part of my order, my common sense.

I know it is not cautious to search the places of memory if I don't want to endanger the meaning, feeble and distant, that those days still have. I must never look for the places of memory in real sites. There is a relationship with one's own falsehoods that could never bear any type of existence beyond the mind. I look at the sky, I see the clouds moving like noiseless trains. The sky is the only thing of which I can say that it is – despite Heraclitus – the same as in childhood. Illusion is the sky's strength. I mistrust memories, just as I mistrust sex, but both tie me to life. We always mistrust the most important things, it's our cowardice.

Beyond the *mezzo del cammin*, life also gets us used to the presence of distances, whether we look backwards or forwards. This becomes more and more evident as we grow older, of course, until one day we realise that the distances have gradually disappeared and that wherever you look everything is equally close. It is not an uncomfortable feeling at all, because it means that after a life of playing against so many forces one begins to have one of the most powerful forces on one's side, namely indifference.

But indifference in the sense of a lack of feeling in favour or against, and thus applicable to a person as much as to a star. Not indifference in the sense of an absence of interest, which is close to the meaning of the word selfishness. The indifference I refer to avoids the anxiety about that which is not fundamental and for that which is inevitable, that which, being important and even transcendental, we will never be able to change. A neighbour of lucidity, it liberates us precisely from what is superfluous and from what is useless.

So far, poetry has been my life, and it continues to be so. Nothing has had power over me if I have been allowed to write. The circumstances that without poetry would have weakened me have made me stronger. The language I speak and the language in which I write poems are the same. So did the poets from whom I learned this, like Gabriel Ferrater or Philip Larkin. Others, on the contrary, have stressed the difference between spoken language and the language of the poem, as in the case of Josep Carner. But all of them have taught me that inspiration cannot come from anywhere but one's own life, however distant or odd the poem may seem.

The reading of a poem, which is a very similar operation to that of its writing, is also done through the life of its reader. This is why I think that before doing an erudite reading one should *really* read the poem: leaving on one side significations, interpretations or critical analyses, letting nothing interfere, let alone observations made from places very far from the simple and profound penetration of words in our mind.

To put it differently: it's necessary to be left alone with the poem. This loneliness may be uncomfortable sometimes, and we may then shut ourselves off with the verses, surrounded by a library – real or made of accumulated readings – of literary and philological studies. Then, obviously, there are diverse, perhaps many, possible interpretations, all different from each other, and one would not know with which one to agree. We may leave the real reading for another occasion, or it may happen that we decide to adhere to one interpretation and to consider the poem to be read thus. It's the same thing that can happen to someone who looks at the paintings of a museum while they listen to the flood of information coming from an audio guide: that they finish the visit without having *really* seen the works.

If a poem moves a reader, it does so through their life. And it does so, not through that which is accessory in the moment of reading, but through that which is fundamental. As if each life were a well from which to descend to one single stream. The poet descends from his well: the only characteristic is that a good poem reaches this deep stream while a bad poem does not go deep enough, it remains too high, dry.

Even if they are not very learned, if a person feels with emotion that what they have read expresses some aspect of their conscience or of their life, then this person has understood the poem. It is for this reason that a poet will always be wise to listen to and to consider an observation about a poem, whoever it may be coming from, as long as it originates from this kind of reading. Because anyone who reads a poem in this manner is using their most noble faculties on the highest level. Incidentally, in this book I have to thank Mariona Ribalta, Pilar Senpau, Ramón Andrés, Luis García Montero, Josep Maria Rodríguez, Mercè Ubach and Jordi Gracia for readings of this kind. And, especially, in this English edition, I have to thank the poet, Anna Crowe, my friend and translator. If the best of me is in my poems, she has always managed to convey this to English readers.

Poetry is the form of expression that least resorts to artfulness, ornament, the one that is farthest from persuasion or from the trickery of pretending to offer what it does not offer. A poem does not manifest itself anywhere but in relation to the life of whoever is reading it, and the poet will have only been its first reader. Knowledge and culture act in the long term, they impregnate and change the person, leaving them in a state of reception more powerful and refined. But good teachers know that if someone approaches a poem with the help not of their own life (and therefore of their formation) but only with the help of information, then this person has not yet begun reading the poem.

We must stay alone with the poem, that is, stay alone with our own fear and ignorance. To accept that we cannot concretise the order that we are gaining in our interior in anything material. That we cannot say why our strength increases as we read it. All this can cause anxiety and even fright and, sometimes, it makes erudition be understood as a reassuring security net. It reassures but at the same time it prevents us from running the risk of poetry and of feeling its vertigo when a poem speaks to us directly. This is why poetry is one of the most serious resources to deal with morality's bad weather. Its appearance must have been a crucial milestone in the history of humanity. As crucial, for example, as the appearance of the house, of architecture, that liberation of the human being from the cave, a first sign of individuality.

Because that which is impersonal, that is to say objective, cannot help to mitigate the effects of moral suffering with dignity, which is basically caused by loss and absence. No consolation can be of use if it doesn't speak directly to a *you*. This is why, tired of ideologies and abstractions, to suddenly encounter a force that works, without any kind of intermediary, on our subjectivity, that accesses the centre of sadness, which is what poetry does, can be so important. If our interests are only occupied by issues like politics, it means that we are putting the accent on what is gregarious in us. And everything that is gregarious tends to nourish contempt. Profound admiration, the type that is not mimetic, comes from individuality. That is, from the *you* to whom the poem is addressed.

JOAN MARGARIT
Sant Just Desvern,
September 2010–September 2014